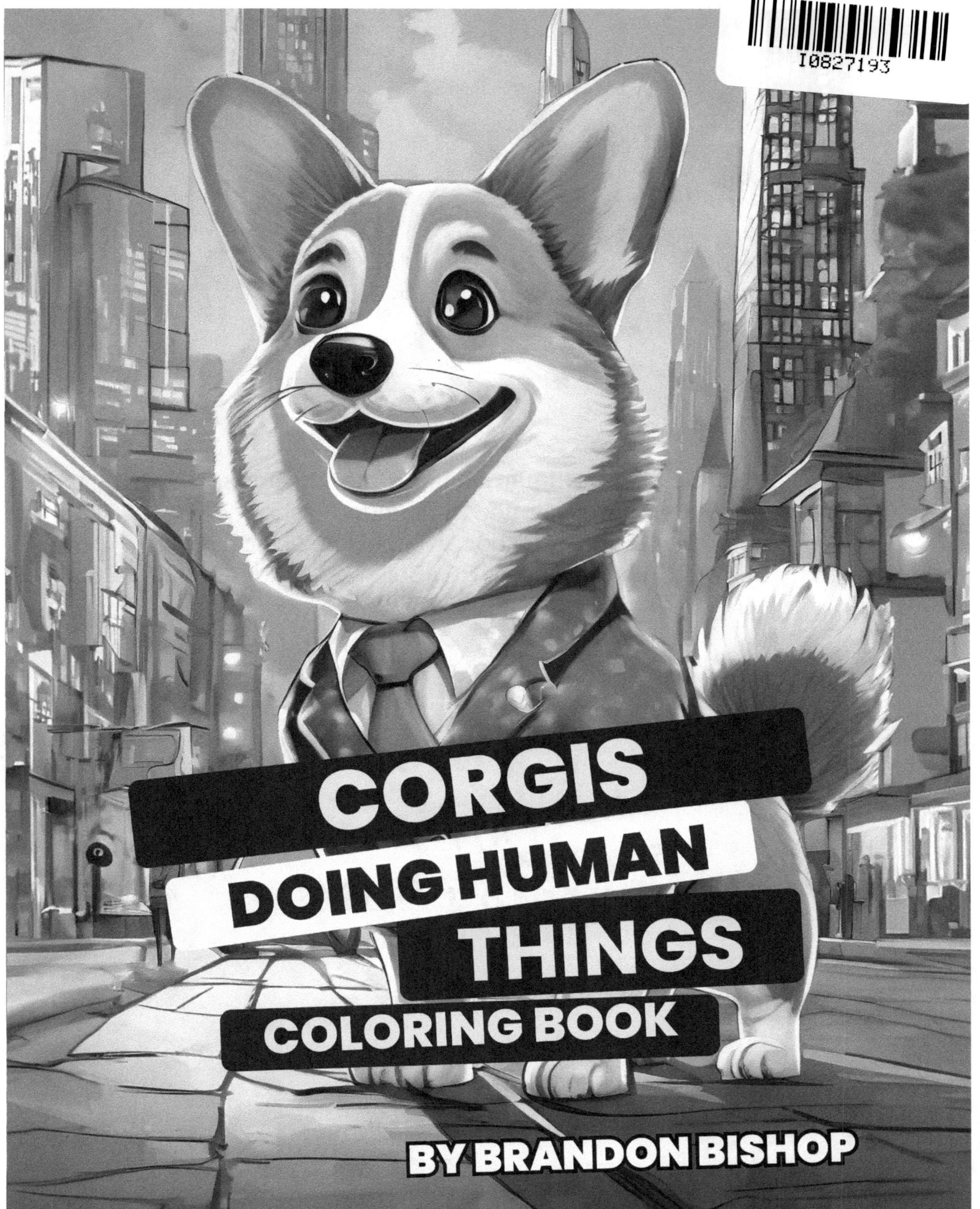
CORGIS
DOING HUMAN
THINGS
COLORING BOOK
BY BRANDON BISHOP

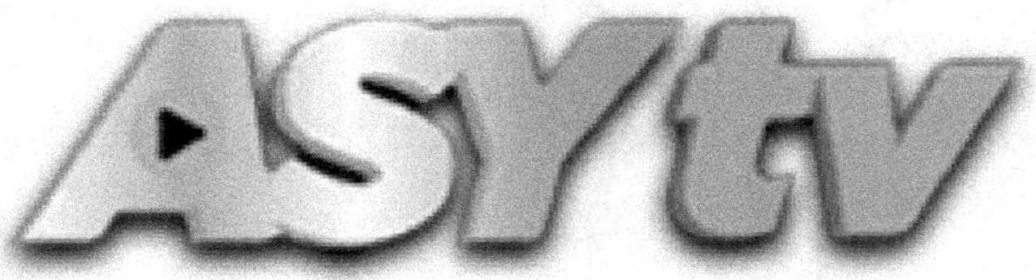

Corgis Doing Human Things Coloring Book
Written and Illustrated by Brandon Bishop

Published by Burning Bulb Publishing, P.O. Box 4721, Bridgeport, WV 26330
ISBN: 978-1-948278-93-5

CORGIS DOING HUMAN THINGS

A Coloring Book by Brandon Bishop

Oh Man… Cuteness Overload! I'm not too sure any of us will be able to finish every image on this coloring book. But for the sake of these colorless Corgis, I know you'll all give it your best shot.

I mean, we've all come this far already; why let the adorableness hinder your efforts?

So concentrate, don't get sidetracked, have all your favorite Corgi colors ready, and bring this super otherworldly Corgi realm to life!!

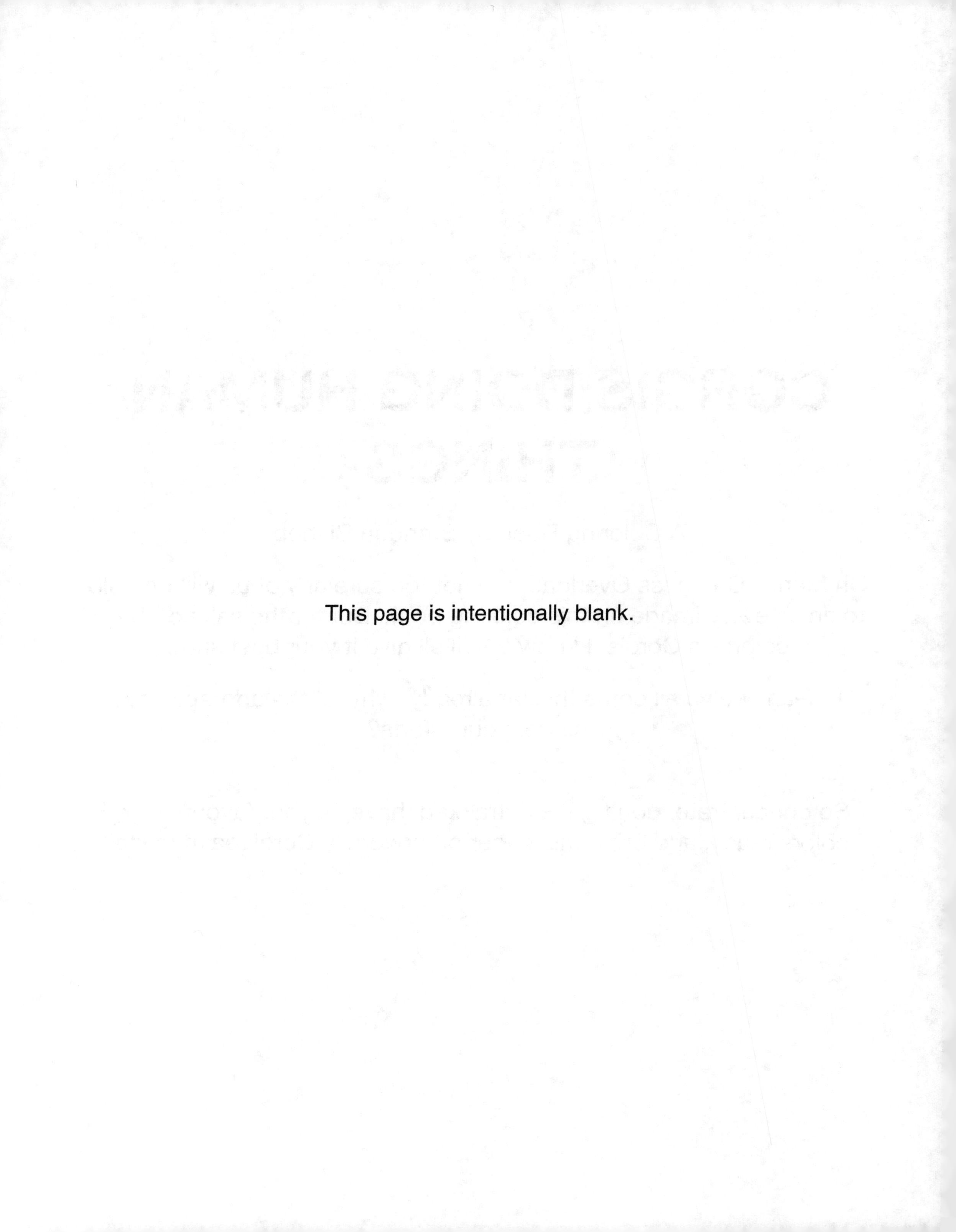

This page is intentionally blank.

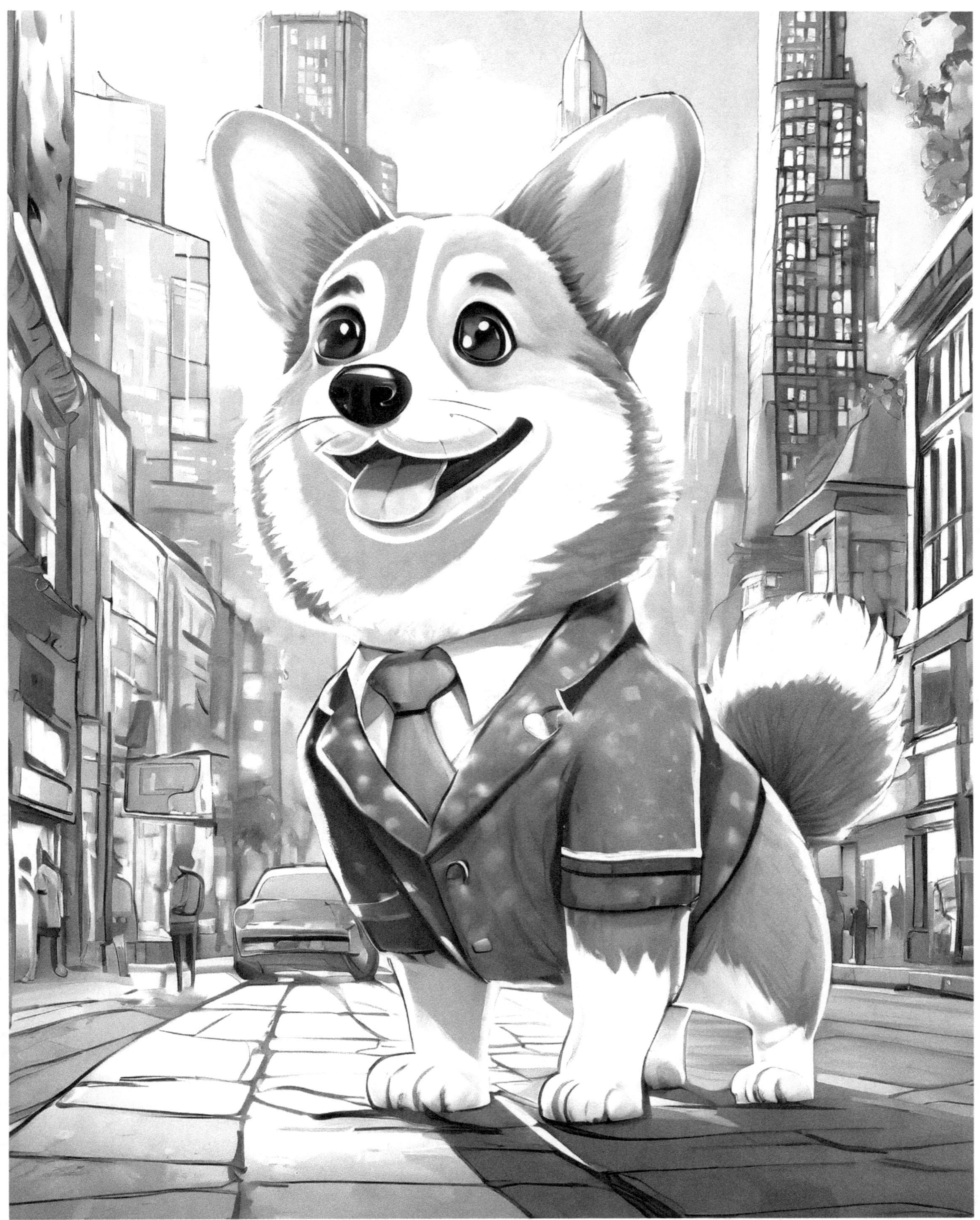

Let's start off with the smartest Corgi in the room. He writes books. He's a Corgi Author. I bet he writes cute things.

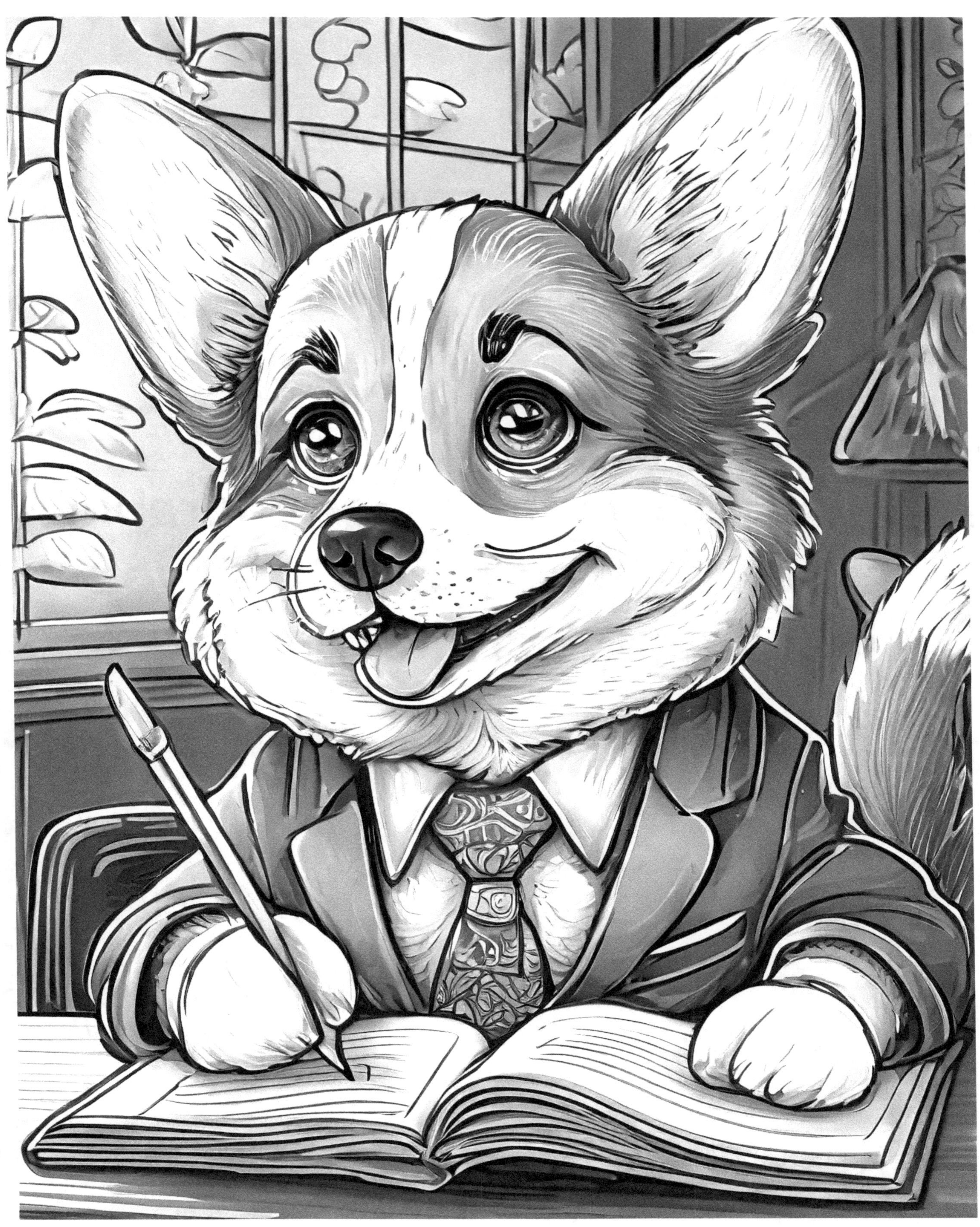

This Corgi is the most adorable clown at the circus. Don’t you just wanna scratch his ears?

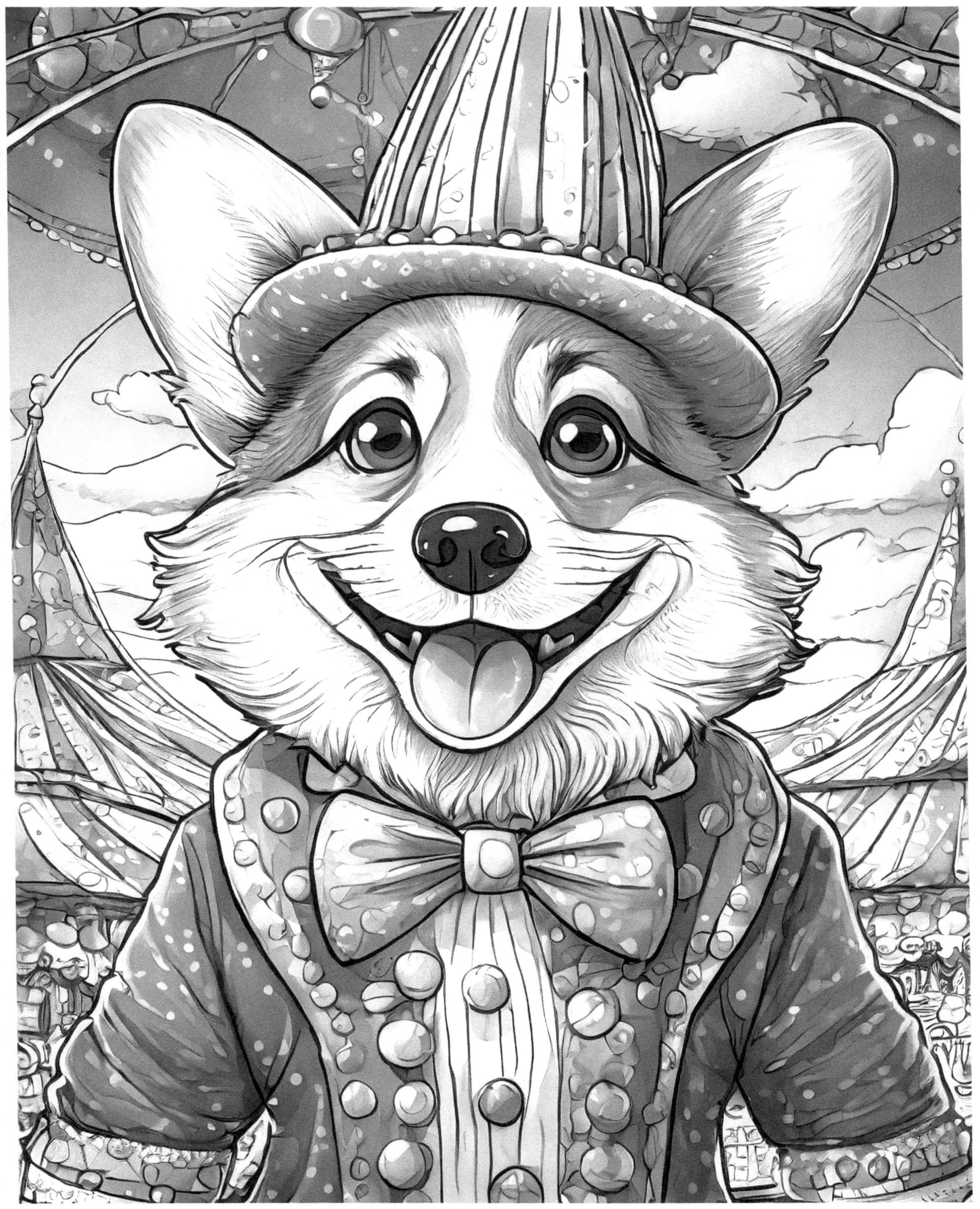

This Corgi does cute magic tricks to astound other cuddly wuddly Corgis.

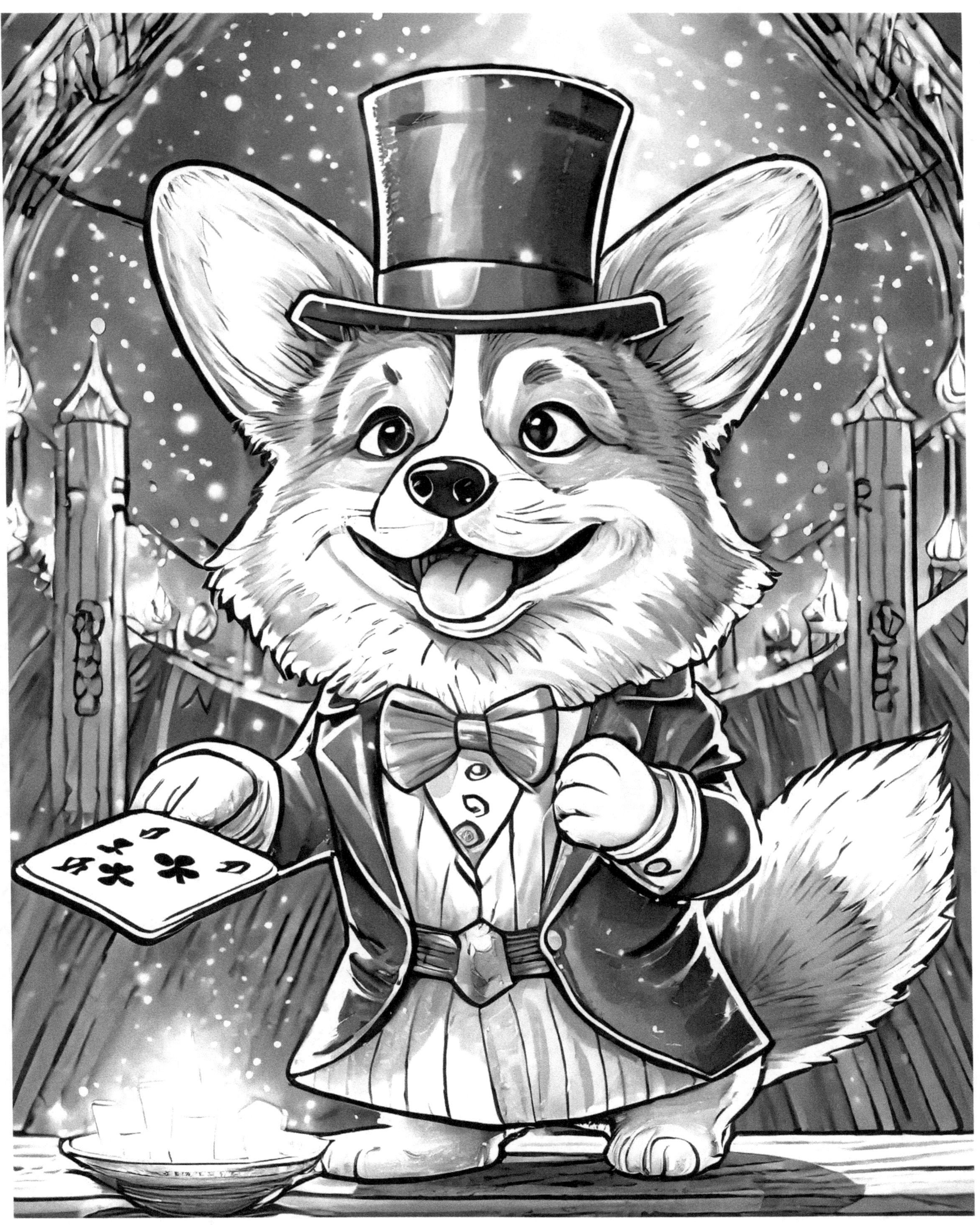

This Bride Corgi is ready to marry the Corgi of her dream.

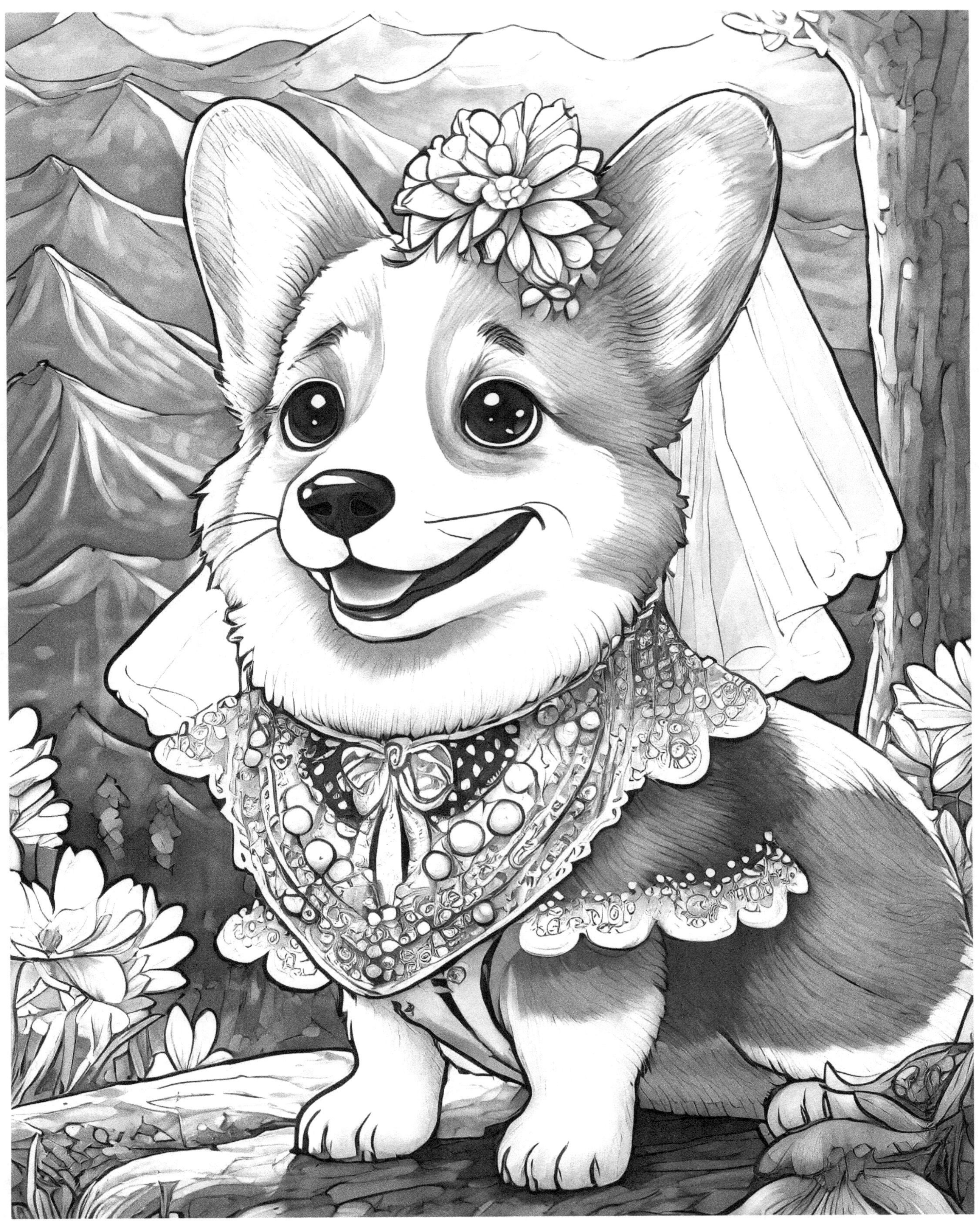

And here he is! The lucky Groom Corgi! I hope they have a wonderful life together!

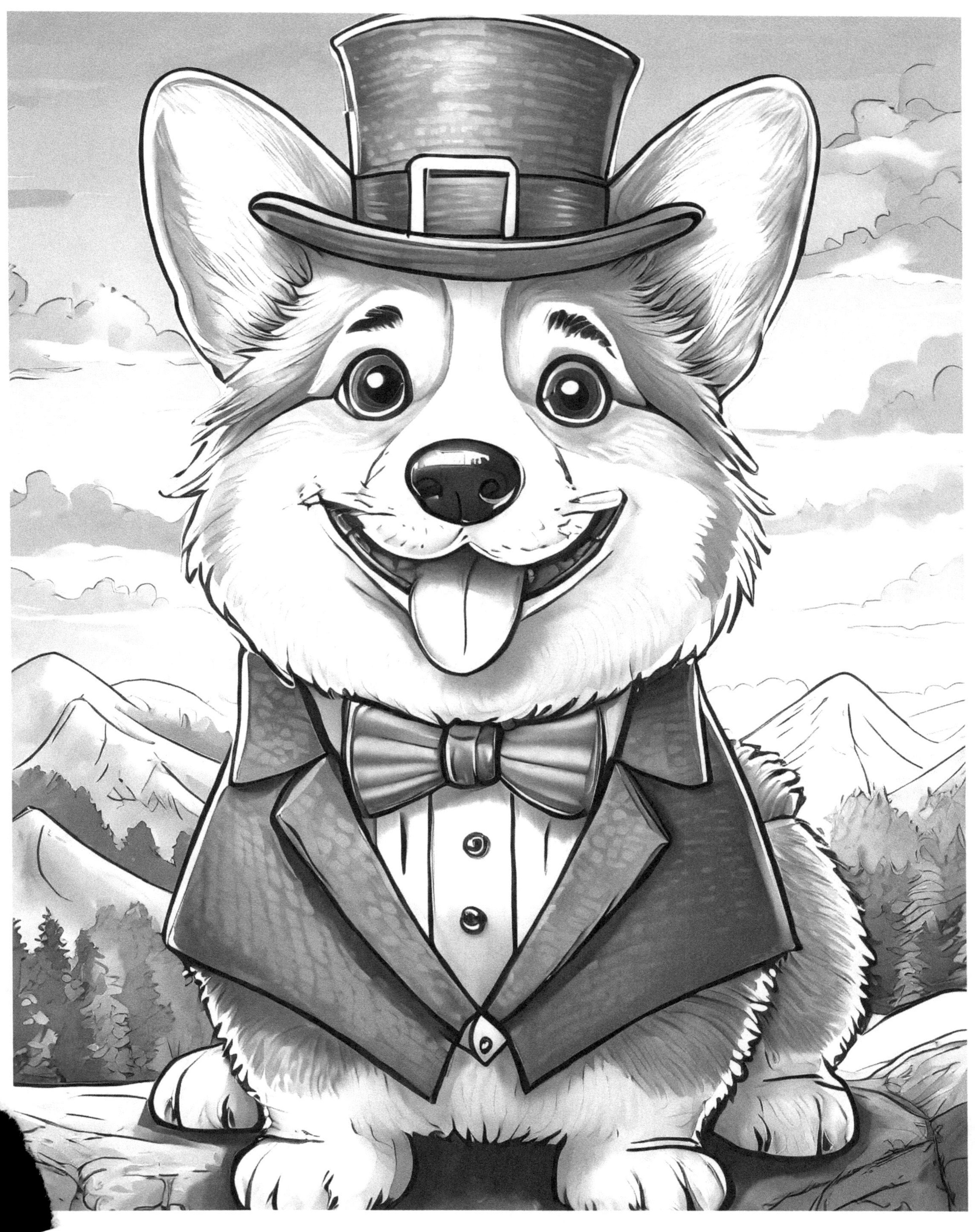

This Corgi loves her garden and all of the fresh veggies that grow there. Now if she could only grow doggo biscuits.

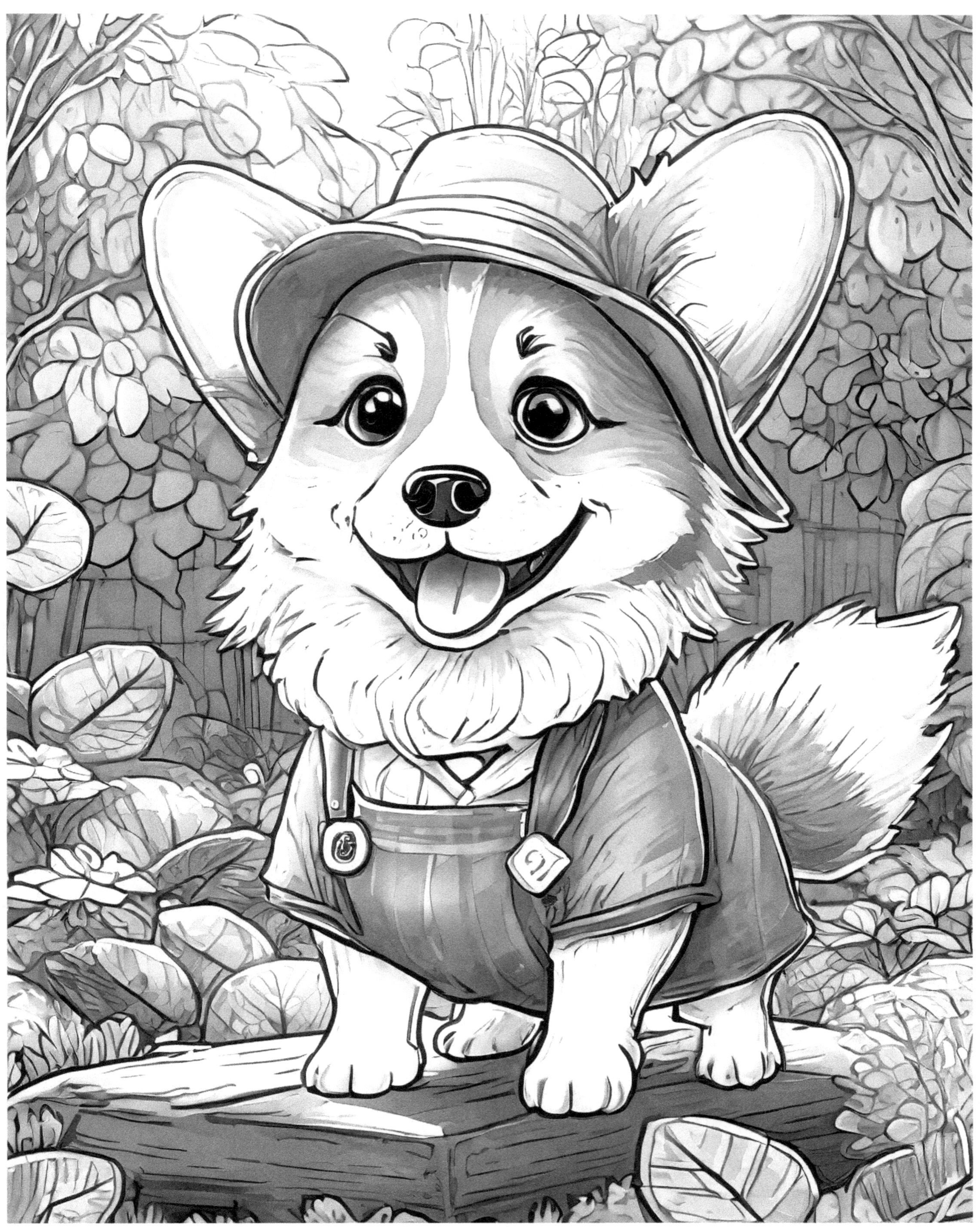

In a Corgi realm long ago, there were gladiator Corgis that fought for fame & honor... and bones.

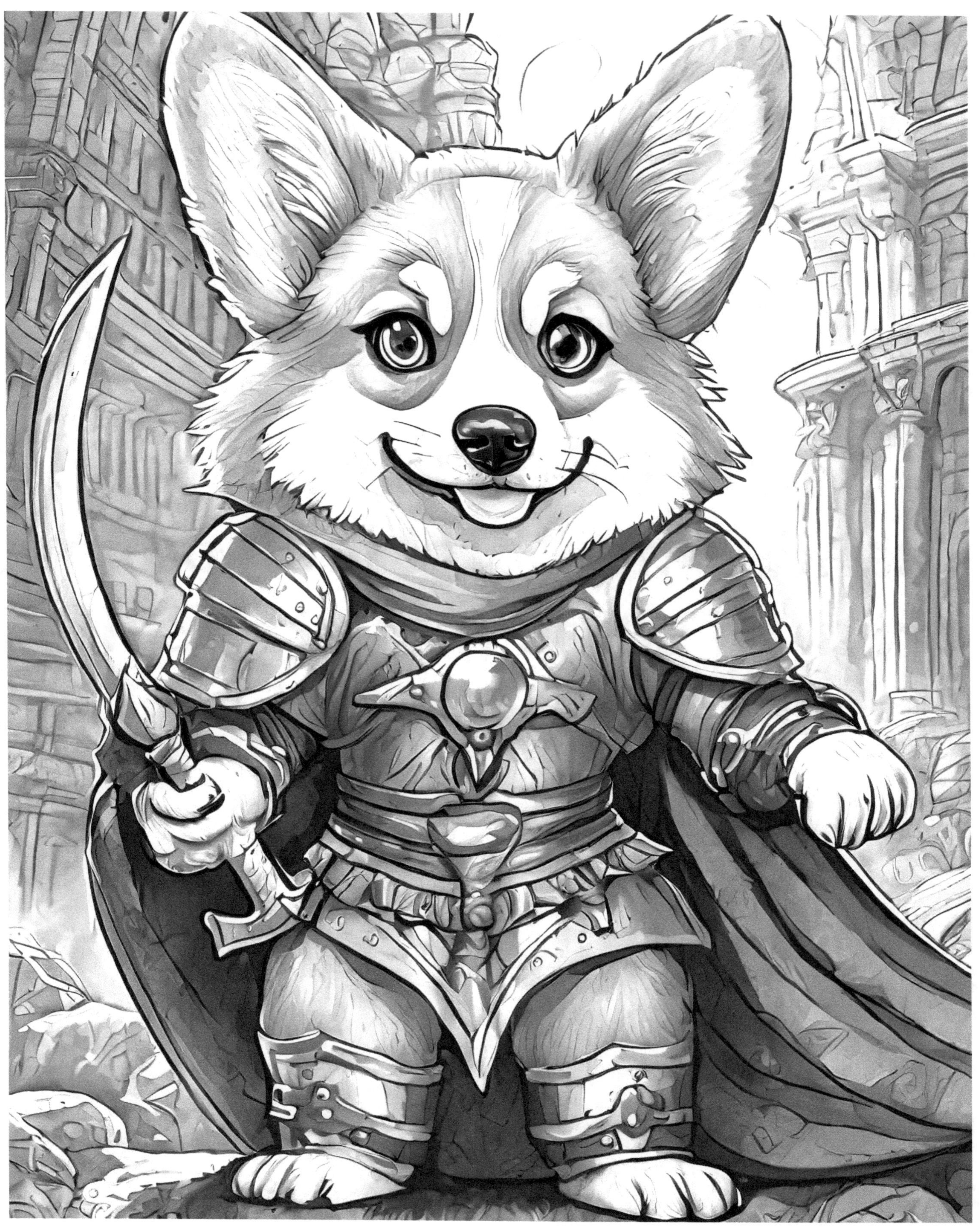

Here's simple selfie a handsome Corgi took out in front of some mountains. He takes a lot of selfies.

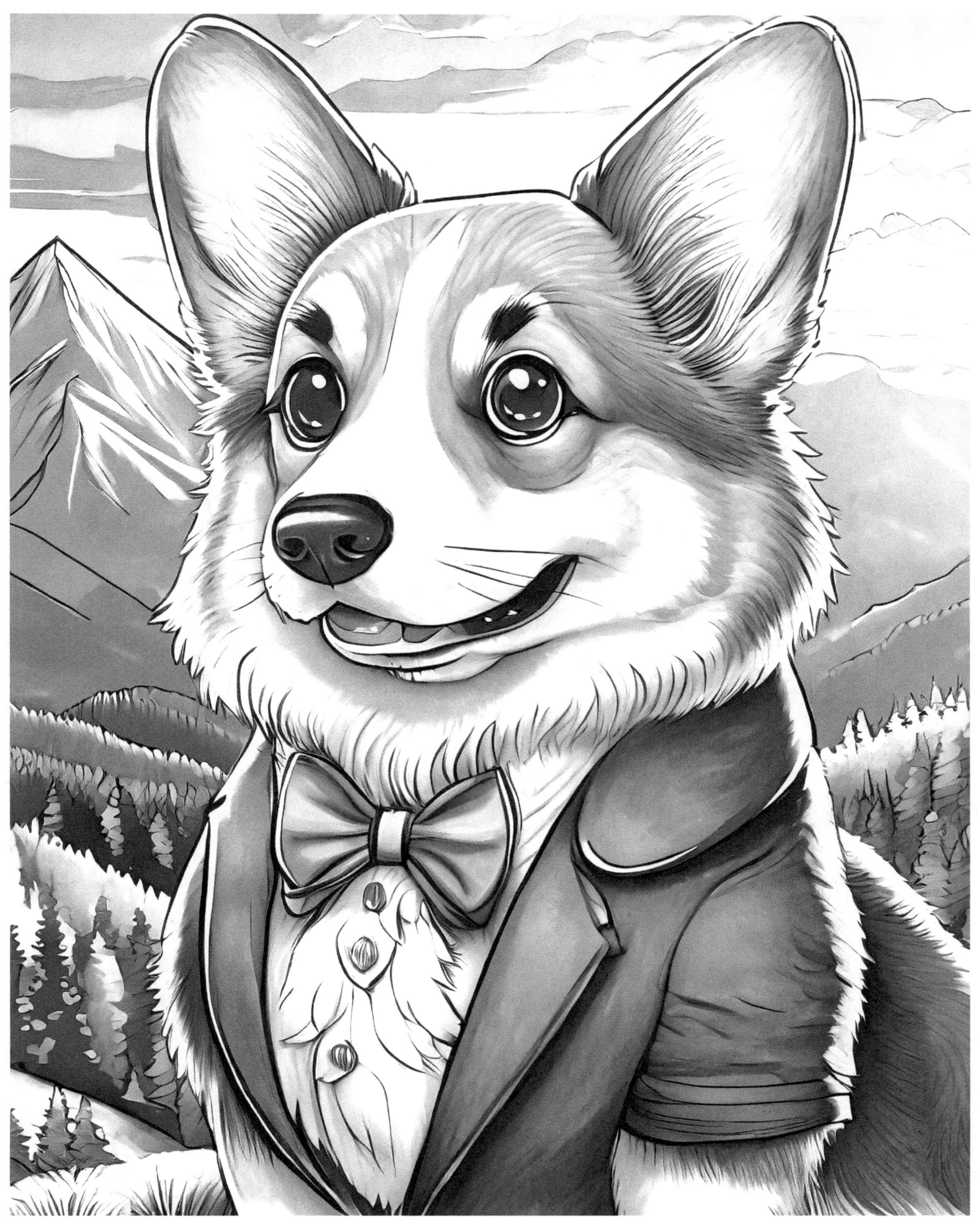

Helicopters need pilots in the Corgi-Verse, and this Corgi is ready to fly.

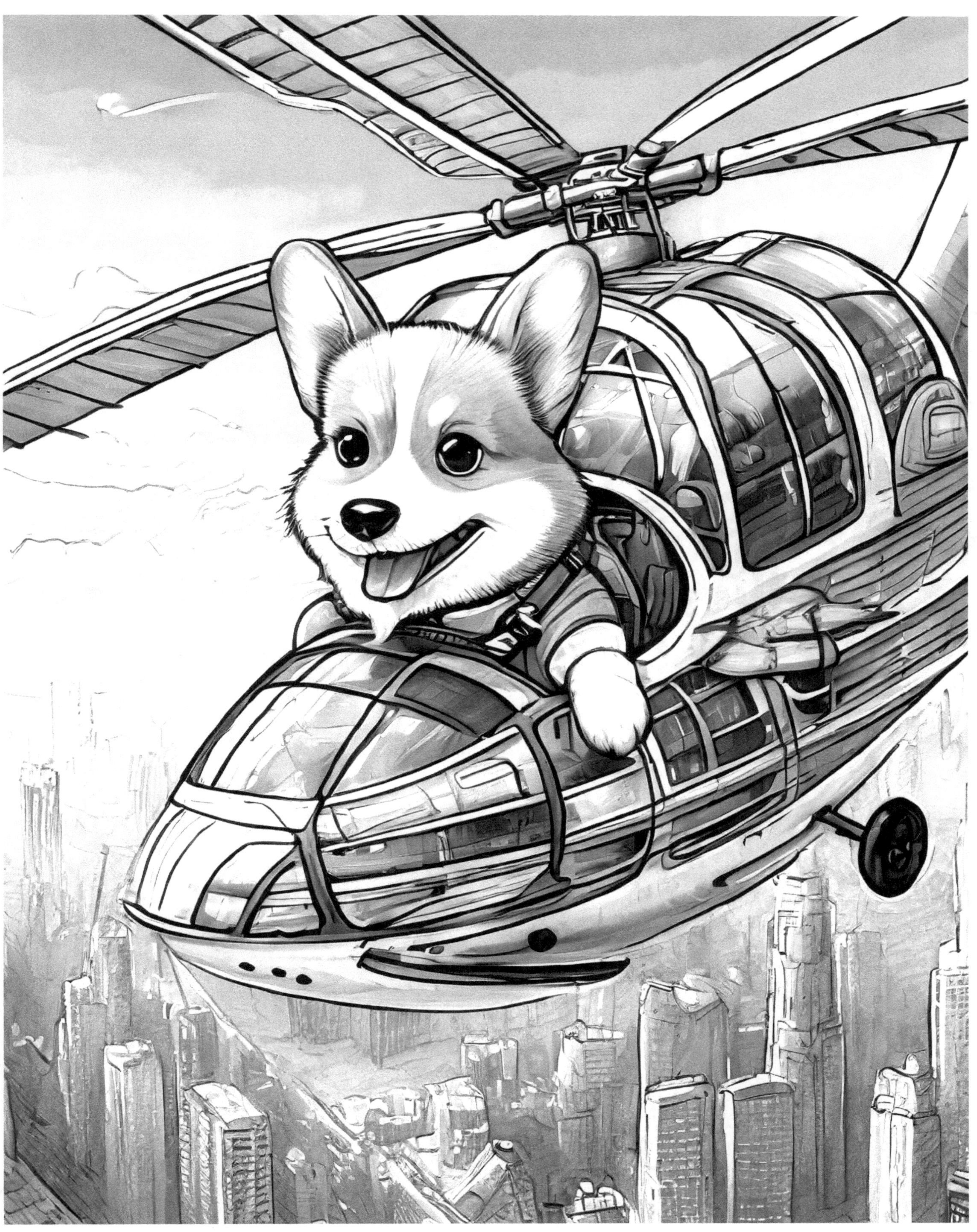

Corgi’s love them some jogging. Especially when a squirrel runs in their path.

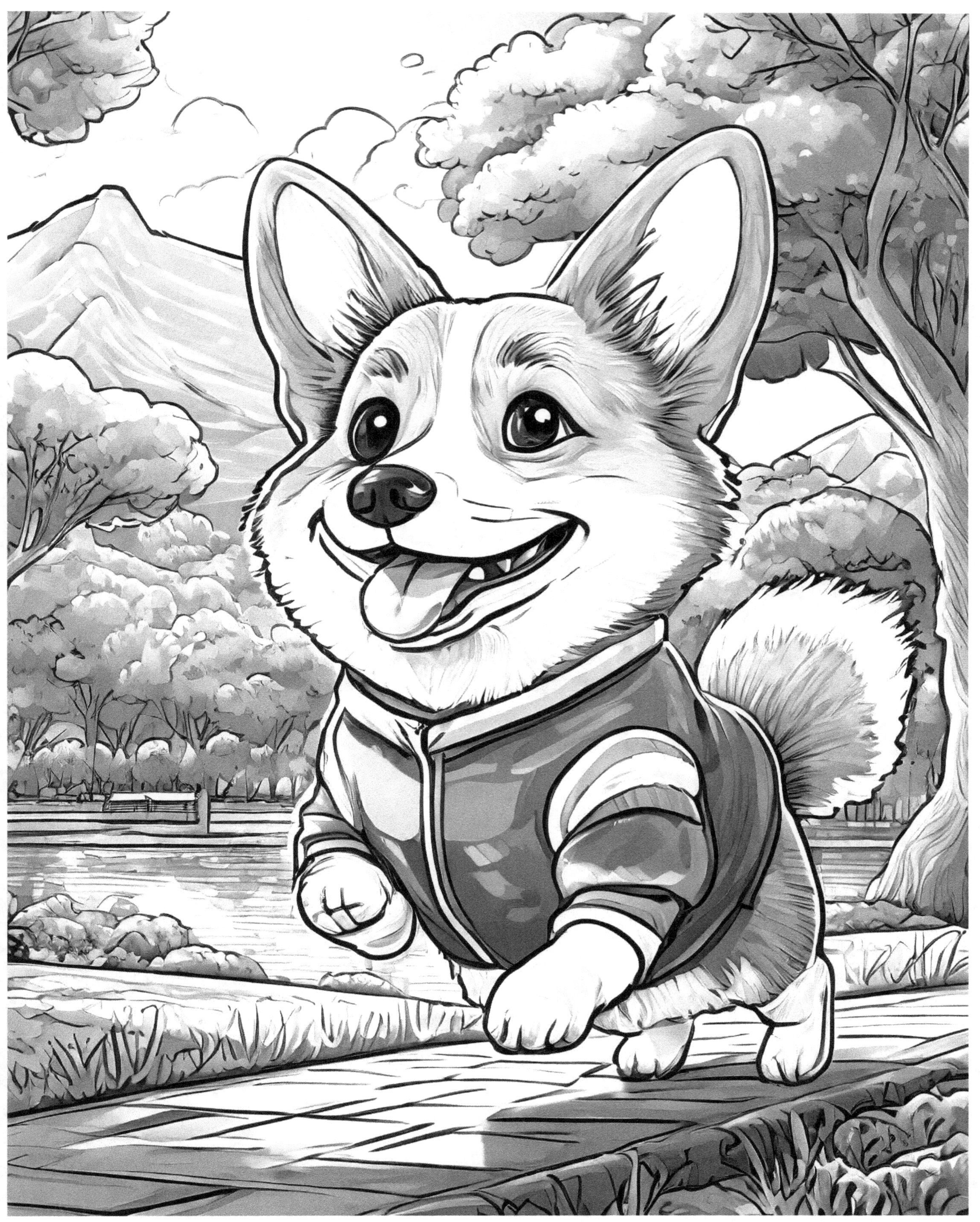

That squirrel got away this time. Corgi's need to learn how to climb trees.

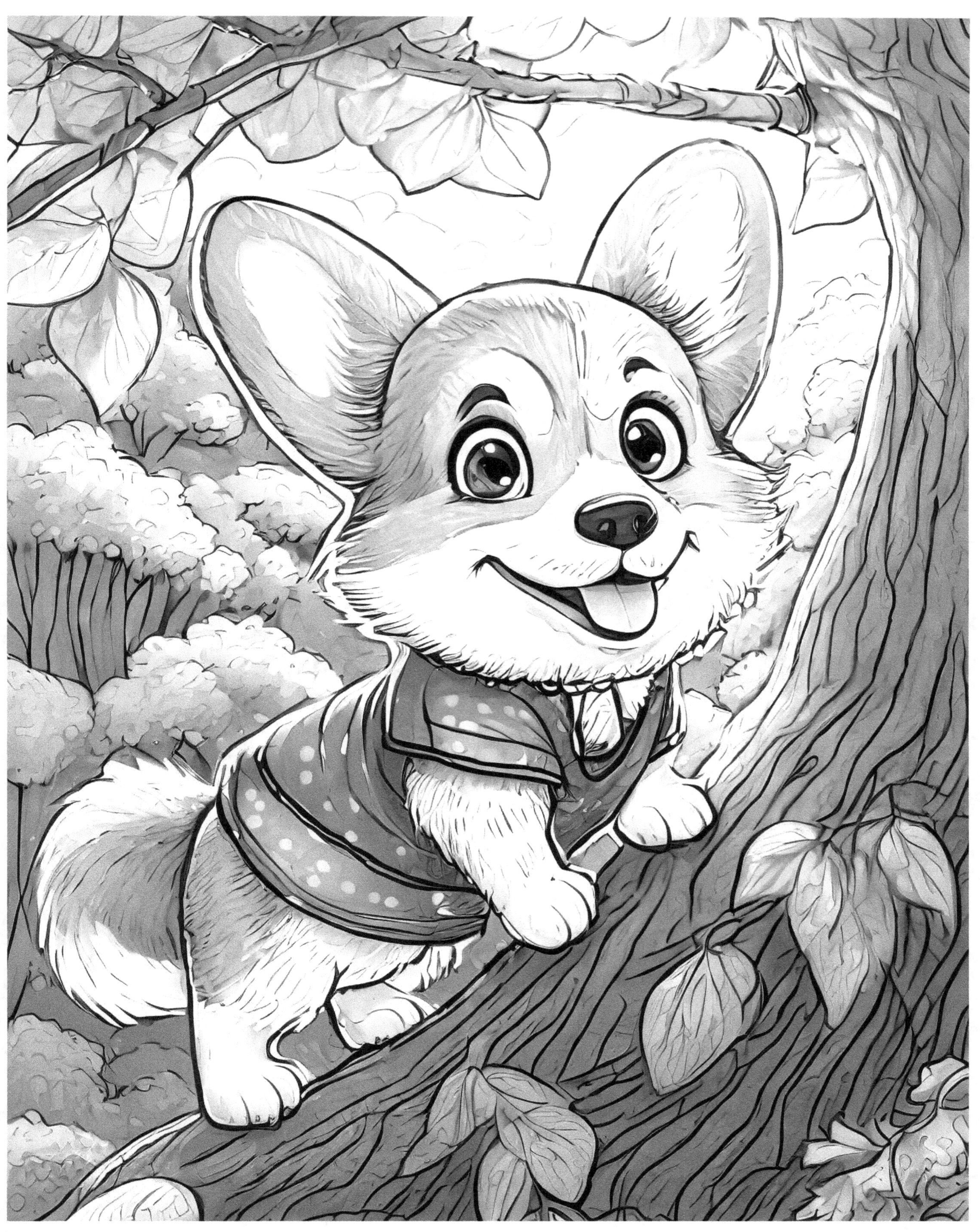

The Corgi kid just got into elementary school. He can't wait to meet his teachers.

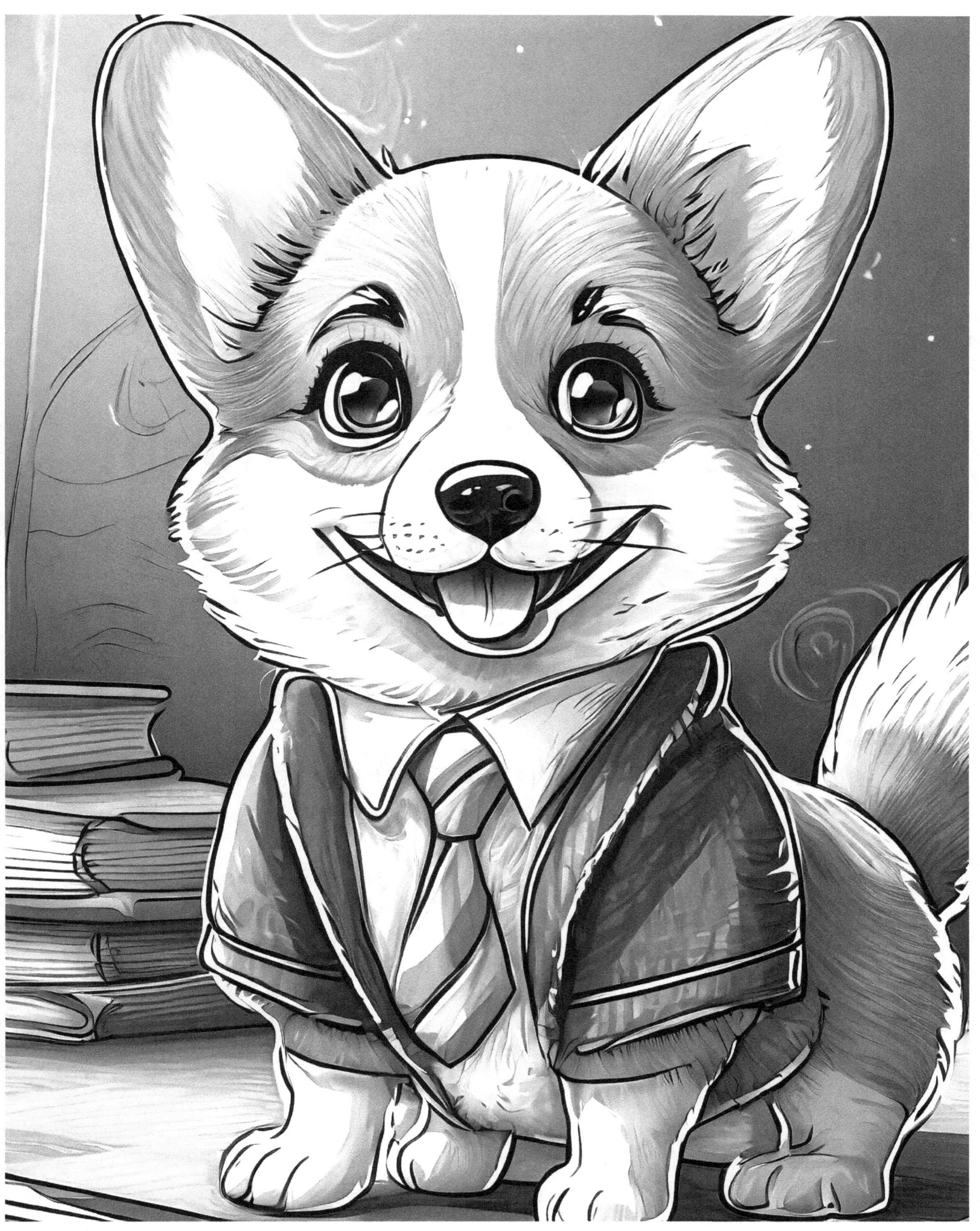

Kings and Queens might be kind of silly in this day and age, but I Corgi history, King's would rule with an iron paw!

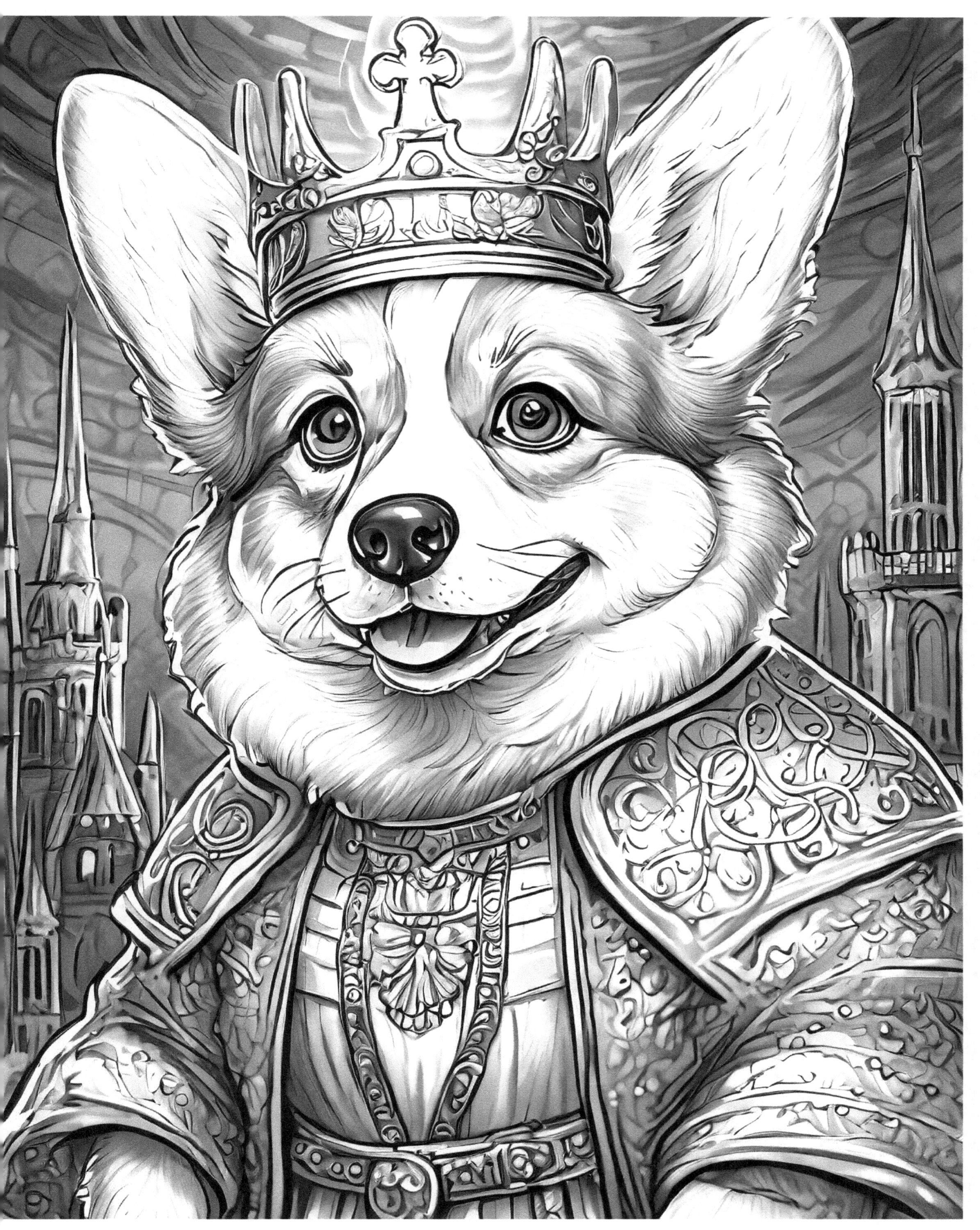

Corgi Queens in history would also lead their nations with grace.

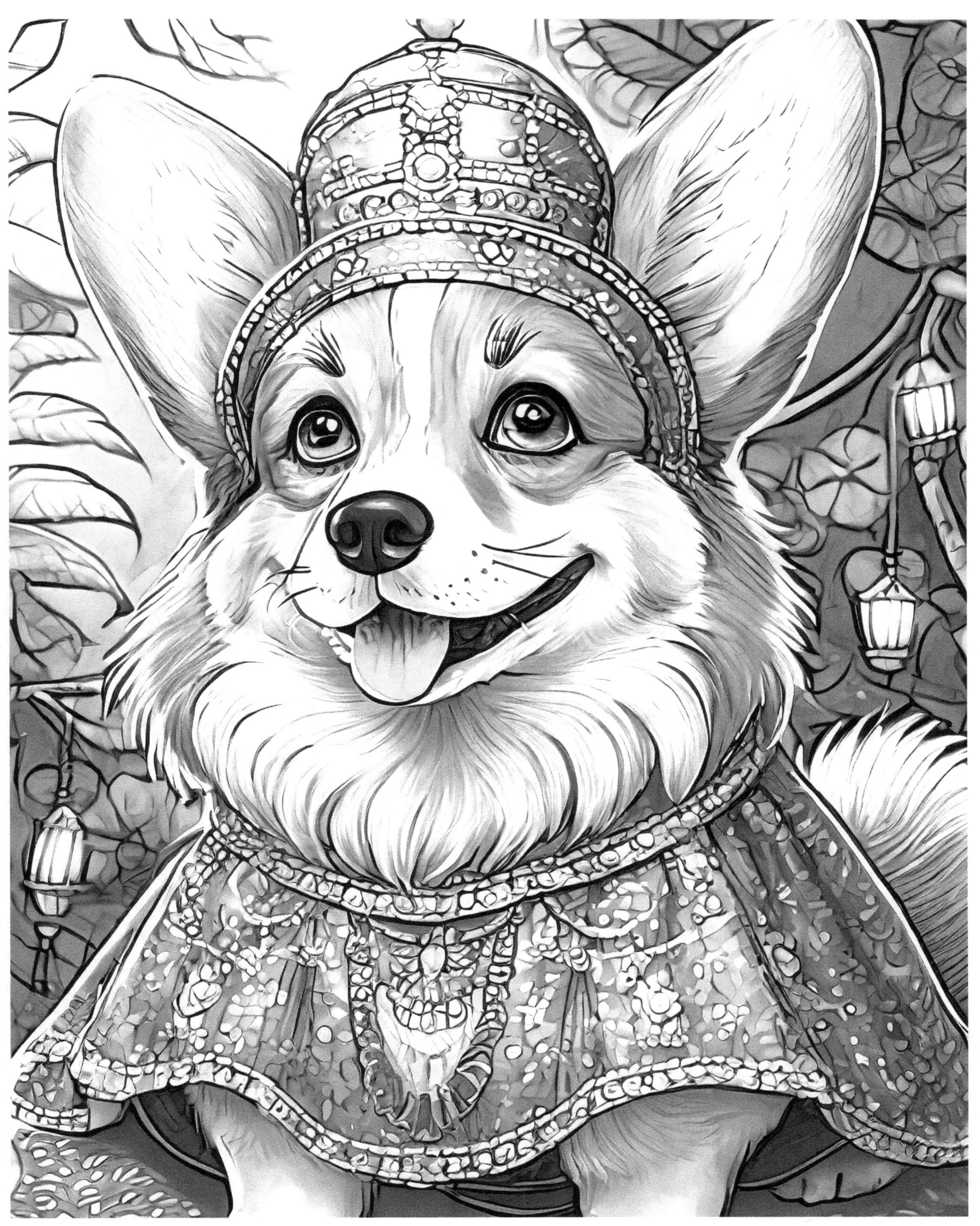

Baseball is a huge past time for Corgis. They usually just run and around and bark and carry the bat in their Corgi mouths, But it looks like fun.

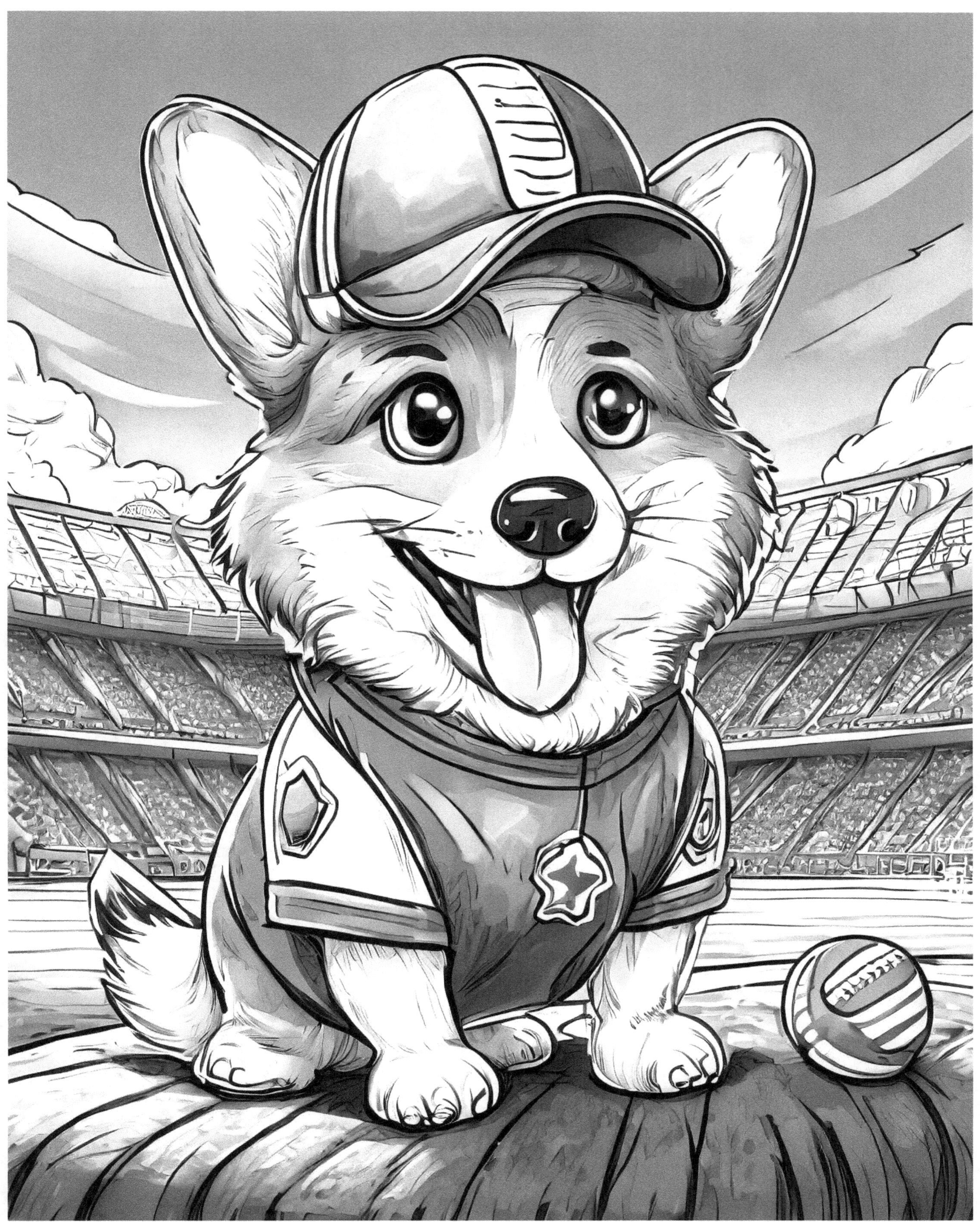

Even in Corgi World,
Coffee is a must!

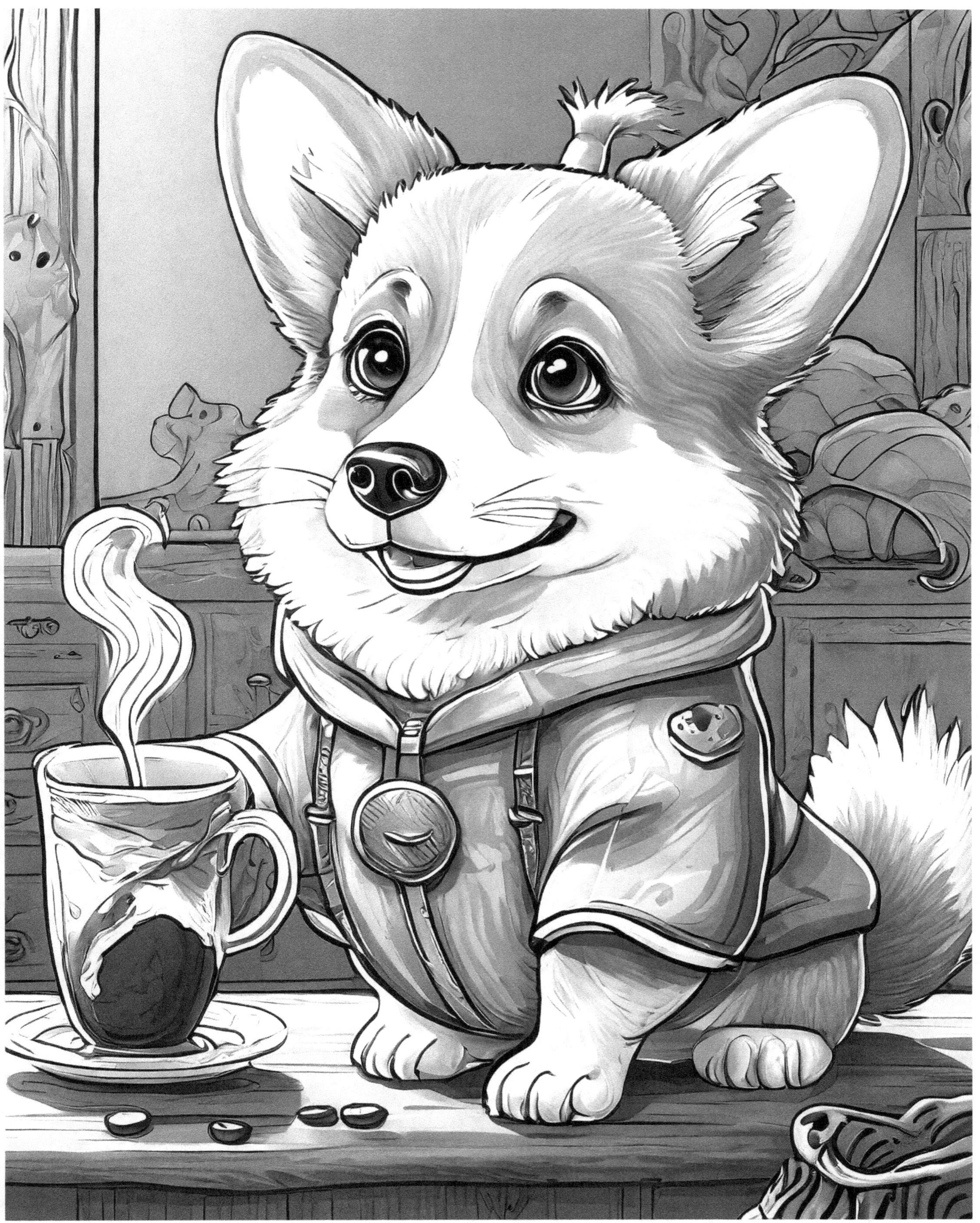

Corgi Cops love doughnuts too. It’s just a thing all cops of any species love.

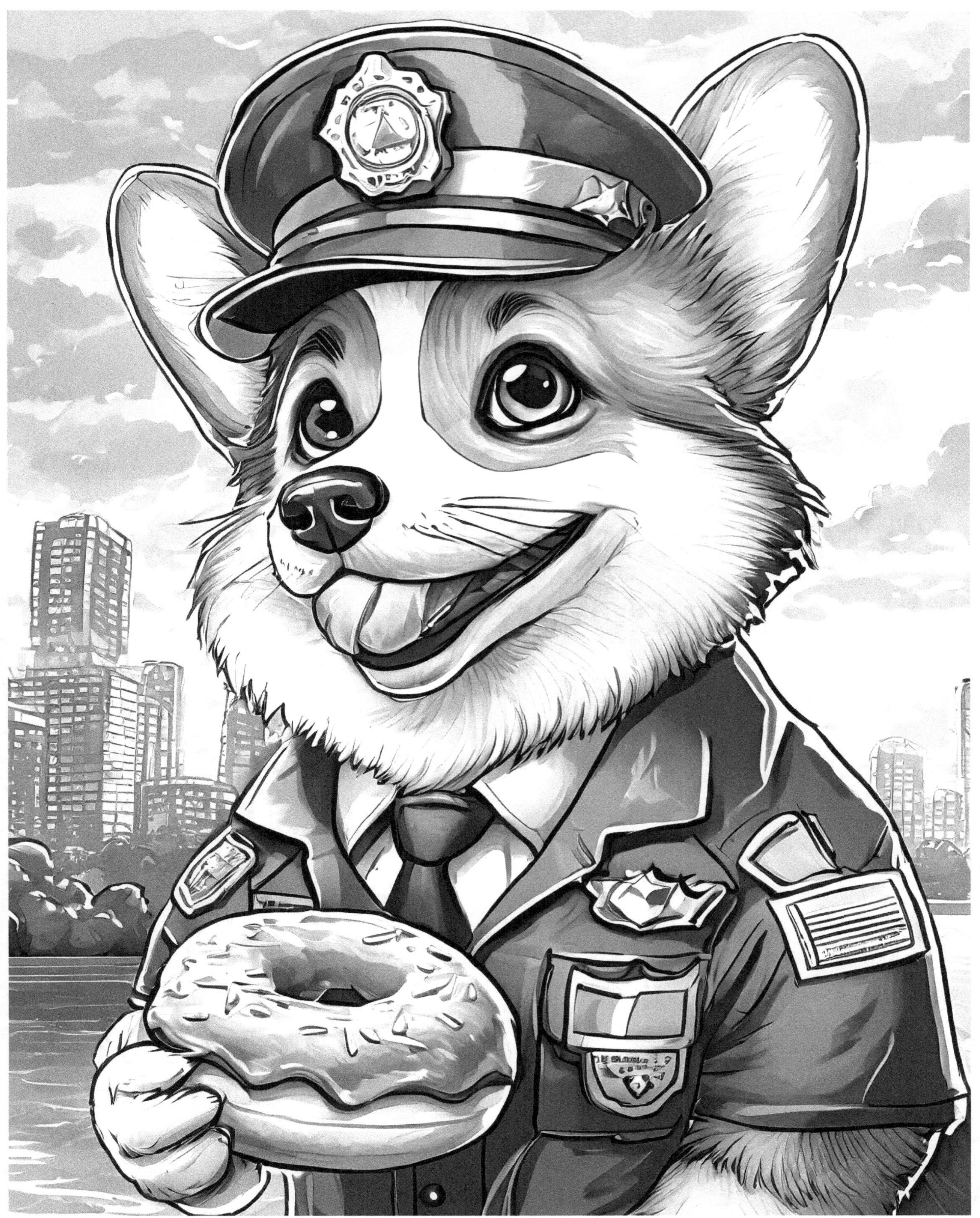

Hard rockin' Corgi drummers lay down the beat!

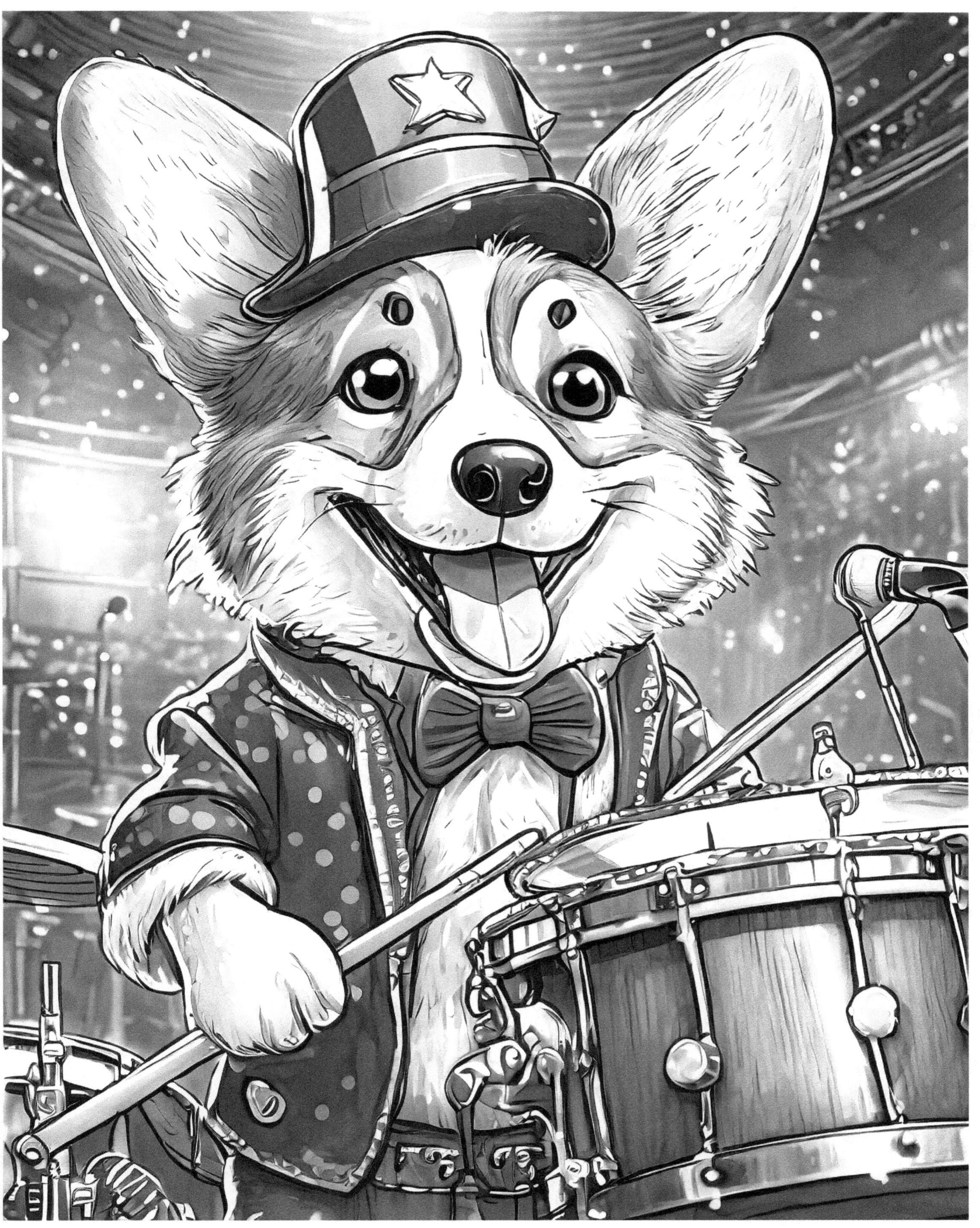

They usually just hang out and chew on tennis balls, but Corgi Tennis is huge in Corgi Europe.

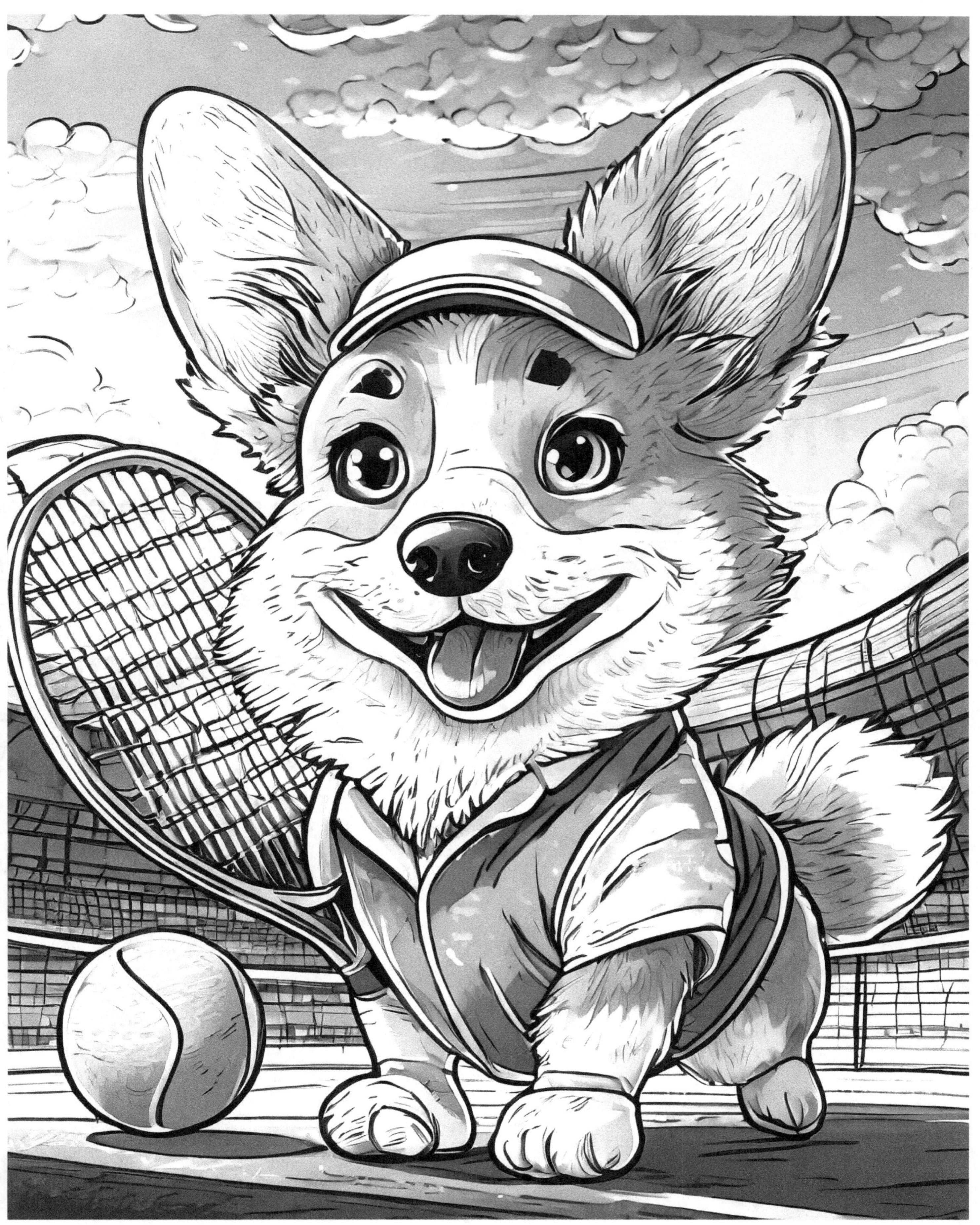

This Corgi is breaking a sweat and putting on 5lbs of solid Corgi muscle! Make sure to have a Corgi protein shake.

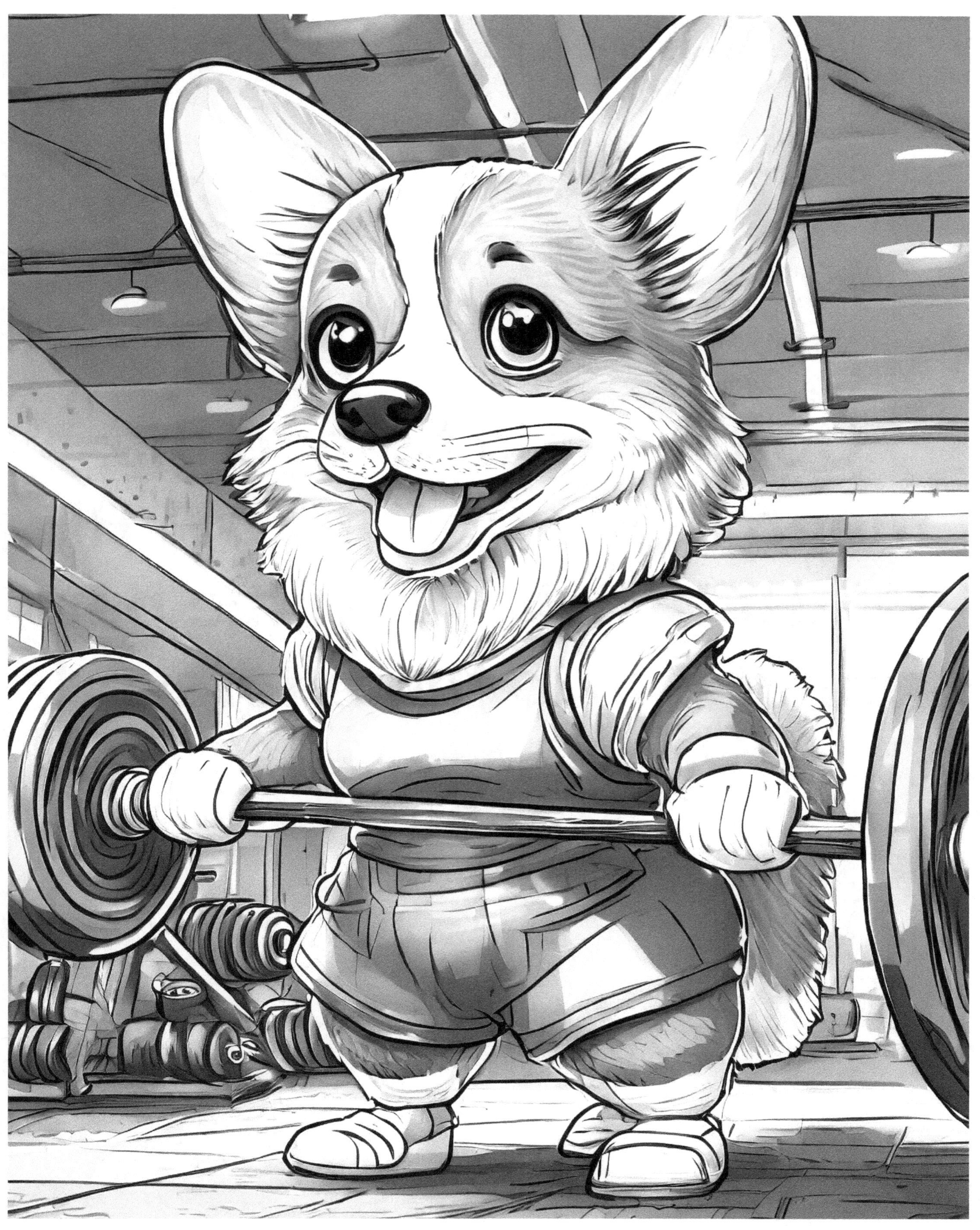

Corgi's didn't stage the moon landing, THEY WERE THERE! Their cute little paw prints are up there forever!

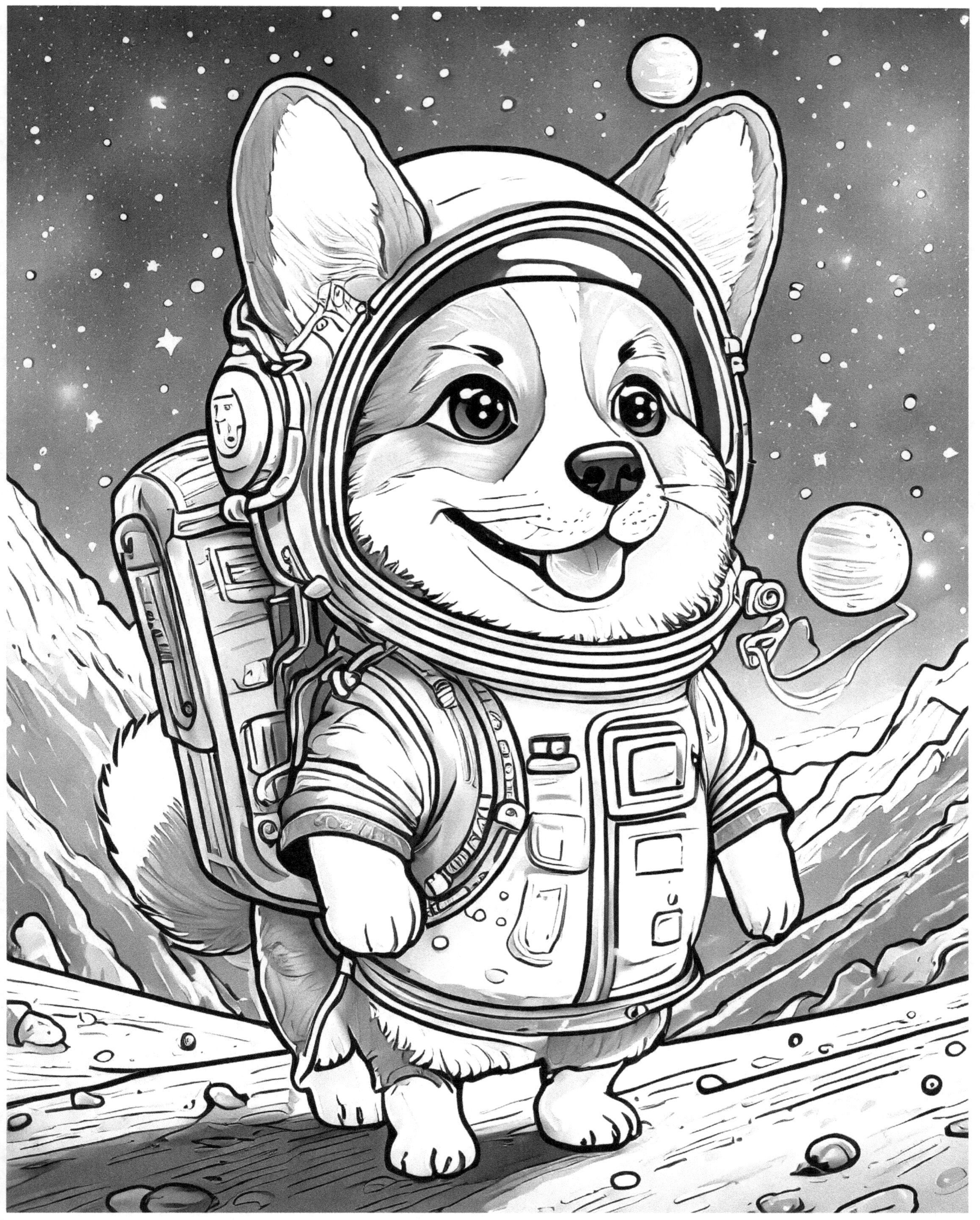

We Did Corgis!!

I'm very proud of us for knocking out the Corgis Coloring Book! And we understand you have your choice of coloring books, so we're grateful that you chose this one!

Where going to get back to animals that actually still exist in the next 7,133 editions. I've heard rumors of Bees, Bats, Deer, Elephants and so many more… Is that okay? Cool!

Written & Illustrated by Brandon Bishop

In Association with ASY TV

ASYTV.COM

ANIMALS DOING HUMAN THINGS COLORING BOOKS

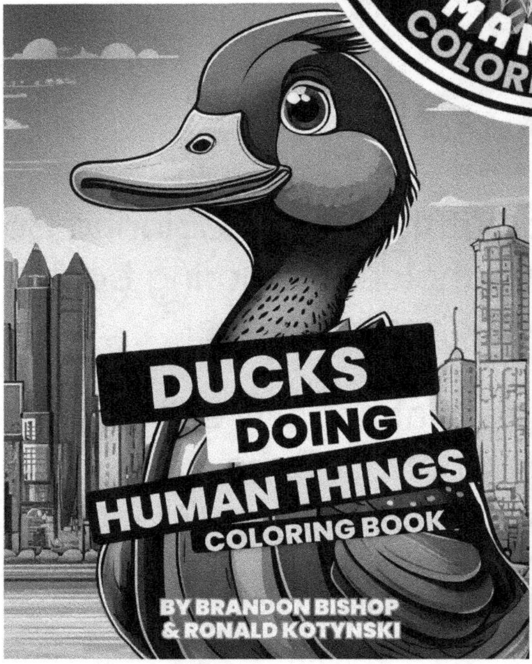

DUCKS DOING HUMAN THINGS COLORING BOOK

BY BRANDON BISHOP & RONALD KOTYNSKI

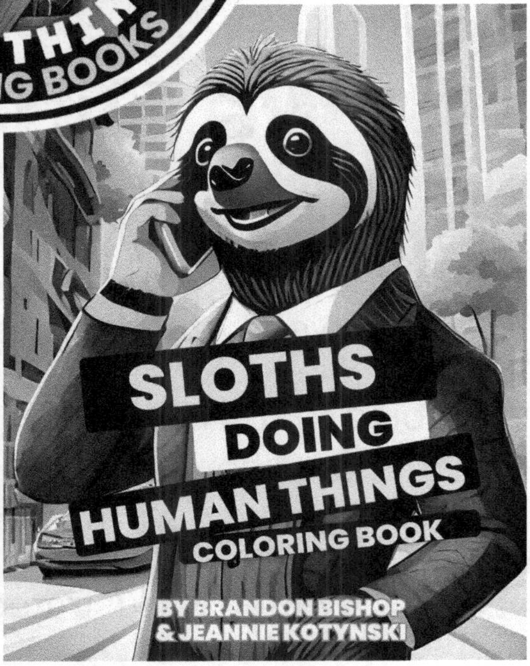

SLOTHS DOING HUMAN THINGS COLORING BOOK

BY BRANDON BISHOP & JEANNIE KOTYNSKI

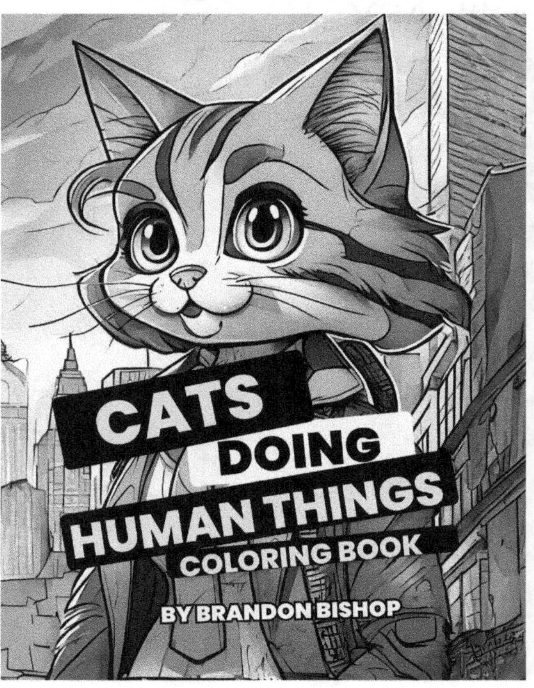

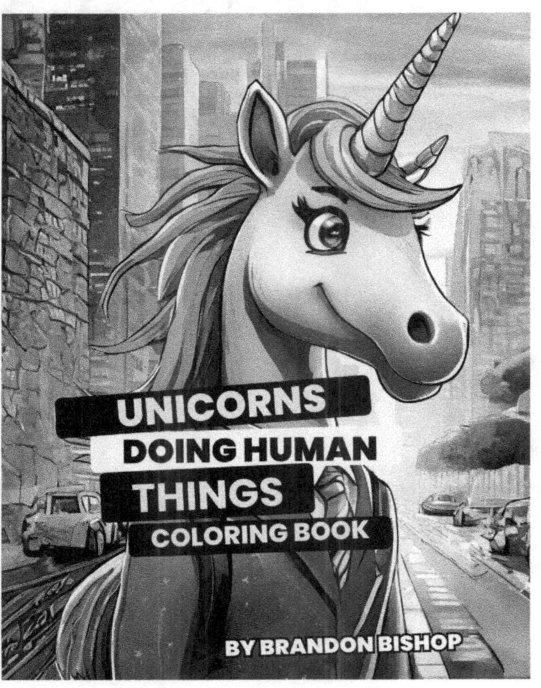

ANIMALS DOING HUMAN THINGS COLORING BOOKS

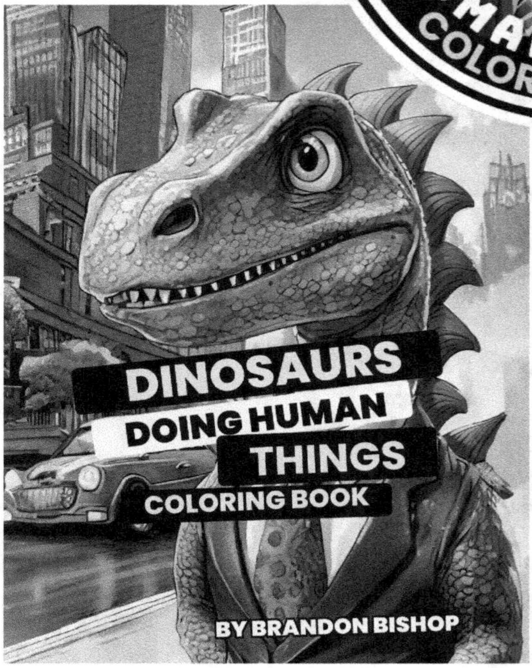

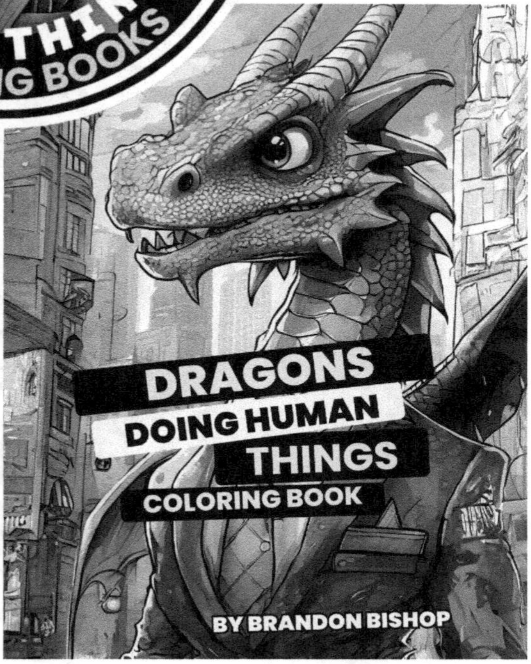

DINOSAURS DOING HUMAN THINGS COLORING BOOK

BY BRANDON BISHOP

DRAGONS DOING HUMAN THINGS COLORING BOOK

BY BRANDON BISHOP

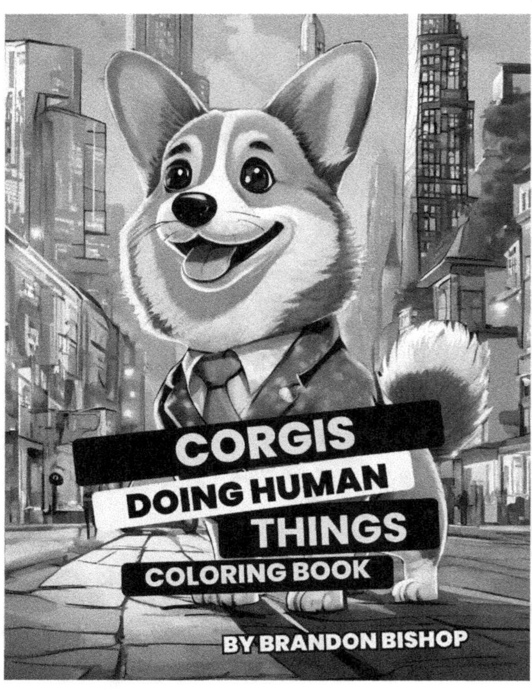

Other great coloring book series from Brandon Bishop:

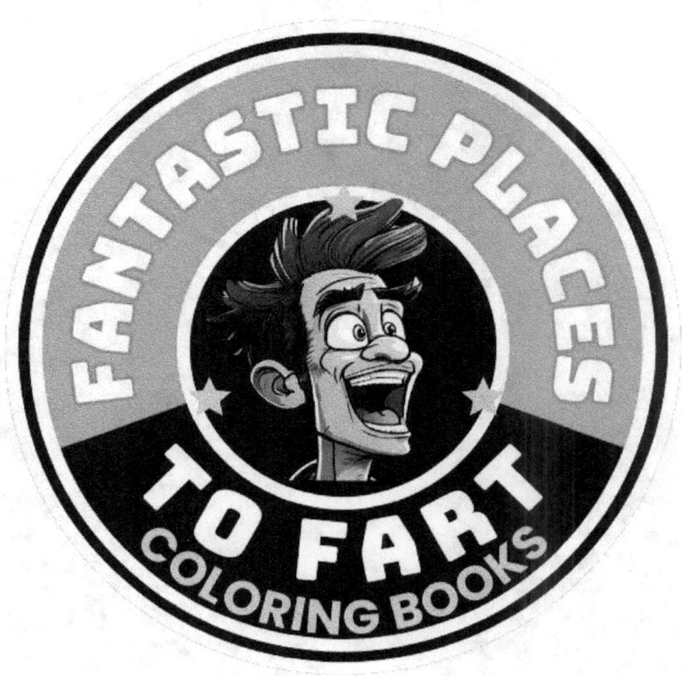

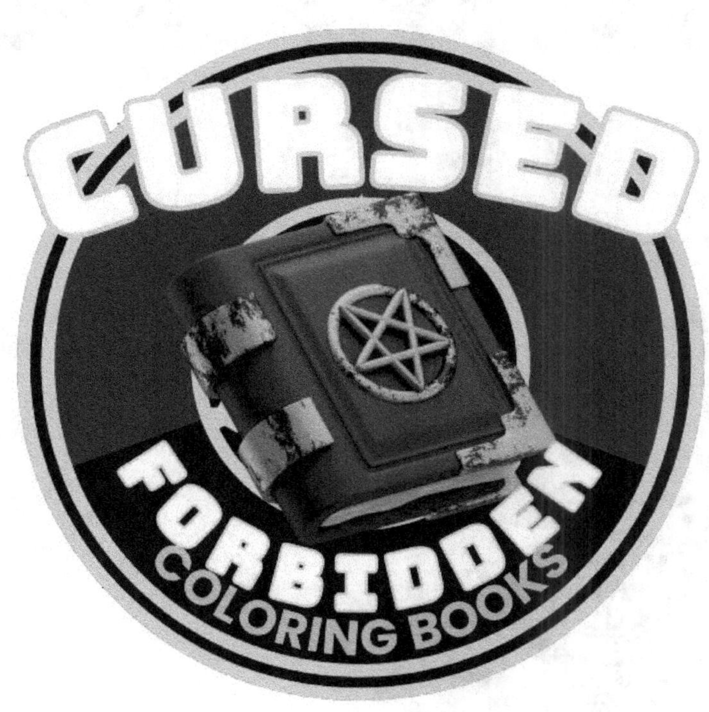

www.ingramcontent.com/pod-product-compliance
Lightning Source LLC
LaVergne TN
LVHW080329110826
845155LV00026B/227

* 9 7 8 1 9 4 8 2 7 8 9 3 5 *